Adult
MAD LIBS

The world's greatest _party_ game

My Bleeping Family Mad Libs

by Molly Reisner

Mad Libs
An Imprint of Penguin Random House

MAD LIBS
An Imprint of Penguin Random House LLC

Concept created by Roger Price & Leonard Stern

Cover art printed by permission of the Norman Rockwell Family Agency
Copyright © 1943 The Norman Rockwell Family Entities

Published by Mad Libs,
an imprint of Penguin Random House LLC,
345 Hudson Street, New York, New York 10014.
Printed in the USA.

ISBN 9780843172850
8 10 9

Adult
MAD LIBS
INSTRUCTIONS

The world's greatest _party_ game

MAD LIBS® is a game for people who don't like games!
It can be played by one, two, three, four, or forty.

• RIDICULOUSLY SIMPLE DIRECTIONS

In this tablet you will find stories containing blank spaces where words are left out. One player, the READER, selects one of these stories. The READER does not tell anyone what the story is about. Instead, he/she asks the other players, the WRITERS, to give him/her words. These words are used to fill in the blank spaces in the story.

• TO PLAY

The READER asks each WRITER in turn to call out a word—an adjective or a noun or whatever the space calls for—and uses them to fill in the blank spaces in the story. The result is a MAD LIBS® game.

When the READER then reads the completed MAD LIBS® game to the other players, they will discover that they have written a story that is fantastic, screamingly funny, shocking, silly, crazy, or just plain dumb—depending upon which words each WRITER called out.

• EXAMPLE (*Before* and *After*)

" _____ !" he said _____
      EXCLAMATION   ADVERB

as he jumped into his convertible _____ and
                                                    NOUN

drove off with his _____ wife.
                              ADJECTIVE

" _____Ouch_____ !" he said _____stupidly_____
      EXCLAMATION   ADVERB

as he jumped into his convertible _____cat_____ and
                                                    NOUN

drove off with his _____brave_____ wife.
                              ADJECTIVE

Adult MAD LIBS QUICK REVIEW

The world's greatest _party_ game

In case you have forgotten what adjectives, adverbs, nouns, and verbs are, here is a quick review:

An **ADJECTIVE** describes something or somebody. _Lumpy_, _soft_, _ugly_, _messy_, and _short_ are adjectives.

An **ADVERB** tells how something is done. It modifies a verb and usually ends in "ly." _Modestly_, _stupidly_, _greedily_, and _carefully_ are adverbs.

A **NOUN** is the name of a person, place, or thing. _Sidewalk_, _umbrella_, _bridle_, _bathtub_, and _nose_ are nouns.

A **VERB** is an action word. _Run_, _pitch_, _jump_, and _swim_ are verbs. Put the verbs in past tense if the directions say **PAST TENSE**. _Ran_, _pitched_, _jumped_, and _swam_ are verbs in the past tense.

When we ask for **A PLACE**, we mean any sort of place: a country or city (_Spain_, _Cleveland_) or a room (_bathroom_, _kitchen_).

An **EXCLAMATION** or **SILLY WORD** is any sort of funny sound, gasp, grunt, or outcry, like _Wow!_, _Ouch!_, _Whomp!_, _Ick!_, and _Gadzooks!_

When we ask for specific words, like a **NUMBER**, a **COLOR**, an **ANIMAL**, or a **PART OF THE BODY**, we mean a word that is one of those things, like _seven_, _blue_, _horse_, or _head_.

When we ask for a **PLURAL**, it means more than one. For example, _cat_ pluralized is _cats_.

Adult MAD LIBS — TYPE A MOM

The world's greatest *party* game

MAD LIBS® is fun to play with friends, but you can also play it by yourself! To begin with, DO NOT look at the story on the page below. Fill in the blanks on this page with the words called for. Then, using the words you have selected, fill in the blank spaces in the story. Now you've created your own hilarious MAD LIBS® game!

PART OF THE BODY _____

SILLY WORD _____

ADJECTIVE _____

NOUN _____

ADJECTIVE _____

NOUN _____

ADJECTIVE _____

PLURAL NOUN _____

ADJECTIVE _____

NOUN _____

VERB _____

NOUN _____

NOUN _____

NOUN _____

VERB ENDING IN "ING" _____

NOUN _____

VERB (PAST TENSE) _____

VERB ENDING IN "ING" _____

NOUN

Adult MAD LIBS® TYPE A MOM

The world's greatest _party_ game

Have you been scratching your _____, wondering if your mom

PART OF THE BODY

has a type A personality? If you answer "_____, yes!" to one or

SILLY WORD

more questions below, your _____ mom is most definitely a

ADJECTIVE

raging control _____.

NOUN

1. In _____ school, if you didn't bring home a report

ADJECTIVE

   _____ full of _____ As, did she lecture you on

NOUN · ADJECTIVE

   the importance of getting good _____ so you will one

PLURAL NOUN

   day be accepted to her dream _____ League college—

ADJECTIVE

   _____-ton University?

NOUN

2. Does she micro-_____ your time down to the last milli-

VERB

   _____? When you were a little _____, did she

NOUN · NOUN

   make you a minute-to-_____ schedule for the weekend?

NOUN

3. If you make the mistake of telling your mom the last name of the

   person you are _____, will she hire a private

VERB ENDING IN "ING"

   _____ and get a full background check?

NOUN

4. If her flight gets _____ for a few hours, does she get so

VERB (PAST TENSE)

   _____ mad that air-_____ security is called in

VERB ENDING IN "ING" · NOUN

   to calm her down?

From ADULT MAD LIBS®: My Bleeping Family Mad Libs • Copyright © 2012 by Penguin Random House LLC.

Adult MAD LIBS

HOW TO HOST A FAMILY DINNER PARTY

The world's greatest _party_ game

MAD LIBS® is fun to play with friends, but you can also play it by yourself! To begin with, DO NOT look at the story on the page below. Fill in the blanks on this page with the words called for. Then, using the words you have selected, fill in the blank spaces in the story. Now you've created your own hilarious MAD LIBS® game!

ADVERB _____

ADJECTIVE _____

PLURAL NOUN _____

VERB ENDING IN "ING" _____

PART OF THE BODY _____

NOUN _____

PLURAL NOUN _____

PERSON IN ROOM (FEMALE) _____

PART OF THE BODY (PLURAL) _____

PLURAL NOUN _____

NOUN _____

NOUN _____

NOUN _____

COLOR _____

NOUN _____

VERB ENDING IN "ING" _____

ADVERB _____

VERB _____

ADJECTIVE _____

Adult MAD LIBS

HOW TO HOST A FAMILY DINNER PARTY

The world's greatest _party_ game

If you're hosting a family dinner party, it's _____ probable that
                                              ADVERB

a majority of your guests are certifiably _____ or at least have
                                          ADJECTIVE

a few _____ loose. Avoid a mealtime disaster by _____
      PLURAL NOUN   VERB ENDING IN "ING"

these guidelines on how to be the hostess with the mostest, without

losing your _____! First, put a responsible person, like your
            PART OF THE BODY

_____-in-law, in charge of pouring alcoholic _____.
NOUN   PLURAL NOUN

There's nothing like having your drunk aunt _____ spill
                                            PERSON IN ROOM (FEMALE)

her _____ about her divorce to put a damper on the evening.
    PART OF THE BODY (PLURAL)

Second, never assume a long-standing fight between family

_____ is water under the _____. If your cousin and
PLURAL NOUN   NOUN

his _____ are feuding, seat them at opposite ends of the
    NOUN

_____. Third, if someone starts talking about a sore subject—
NOUN

like your cousin's stint in _____-collar prison or how Grandpa's
                            COLOR

_____ of the month is _____ all his cash—it's up
NOUN   VERB ENDING IN "ING"

to you to _____ change topics. Fourth, act like you love
          ADVERB

having everyone over, even if they _____ you up the wall.
                                   VERB

_____ luck!
ADJECTIVE

MAD LIBS® is fun to play with friends, but you can also play it by yourself! To begin with, DO NOT look at the story on the page below. Fill in the blanks on this page with the words called for. Then, using the words you have selected, fill in the blank spaces in the story. Now you've created your own hilarious MAD LIBS® game!

A PLACE _____

VERB _____

VERB _____

NOUN _____

PART OF THE BODY _____

NOUN _____

NOUN _____

VERB _____

NOUN _____

NOUN _____

PLURAL NOUN _____

NOUN _____

PLURAL NOUN _____

VERB ENDING IN "ING" _____

VERB ENDING IN "ING" _____

ADJECTIVE _____

PERSON IN ROOM (MALE) _____

NOUN _____

VERB

The world's greatest _party_ game

Welcome to your annual family reunion in (the) scenic _____, just
_{A PLACE}

a stone's _____ away from that other place that was too expensive
_{VERB}

for some of us. Here's a partial list of family activities scheduled:

• 9 AM: Rise and _____ and don't forget to wear your name
_{VERB}

tag! Enjoy breakfast with your second _____ twice removed.
_{NOUN}

Remember him? He's the one who never looks you in the

_____ when he speaks. Also, when he does talk, it's about his
_{PART OF THE BODY}

expansive model _____ collection.
_{NOUN}

• 11:30 AM: Don a life-_____ , hop in a canoe, and _____
_{NOUN}   _{VERB}

out on the lake with your brother-in-_____ who loves to brag
_{NOUN}

about his huge yearly _____ and his stock _____.
_{NOUN}   _{PLURAL NOUN}

• 1 PM: Mandatory soft-_____ game! Play with so-called mature
_{NOUN}

_____ who get into _____ matches over runs. Expect to
_{PLURAL NOUN}   _{VERB ENDING IN "ING"}

hear lots of cursing and non-ironic name-_____. This is what
_{VERB ENDING IN "ING"}

good _____-fashioned family fun is all about!
_{ADJECTIVE}

• 3 PM: Photo time! Stand between your uncle who smells like he

bathes in _____ Daniel's or your other uncle who smells like
_{PERSON IN ROOM (MALE)}

a dead _____. Either way, it's a win-_____ situation!
_{NOUN}   _{VERB}

MAD LIBS® is fun to play with friends, but you can also play it by yourself! To begin with, DO NOT look at the story on the page below. Fill in the blanks on this page with the words called for. Then, using the words you have selected, fill in the blank spaces in the story. Now you've created your own hilarious MAD LIBS® game!

VERB _____

PART OF THE BODY _____

NOUN _____

ADJECTIVE _____

PERSON IN ROOM (FEMALE) _____

ADJECTIVE _____

ADJECTIVE _____

PLURAL NOUN _____

ADVERB _____

PLURAL NOUN _____

VERB (PAST TENSE) _____

ADJECTIVE _____

ADJECTIVE _____

COLOR _____

ADJECTIVE _____

VERB ENDING IN "ING" _____

NOUN _____

VERB ENDING IN "ING" _____

THANKSGIVING MENU

The world's greatest __party__ game

It's that special time of year when we gather together to _____
VERB

ourselves silly and give thanks that the _____-ball game is on
PART OF THE BODY

later so that no one has to actually talk to each other. Here's a menu for

today's dysfunctional family feast:

- Butter-_____ squash soup served with cranberry muffins and a
  NOUN

  few _____ looks from Aunt _____, who overheard
  ADJECTIVE   PERSON IN ROOM (FEMALE)

  you say her baby was "definitely hit with the _____ stick."
  ADJECTIVE

- Baked _____ potatoes topped with mini-_____ and
  ADJECTIVE   PLURAL NOUN

  a healthy dose of embarrassment as your mom _____ says,
  ADVERB

  "Aren't you still trying to lose a few _____, sweetie?"
  PLURAL NOUN

- _____ turkey seasoned with fresh herbs and slathered in
  VERB (PAST TENSE)

  _____, awkward silence as everyone watches your sister
  ADJECTIVE

  and her no-_____ husband fight.
  ADJECTIVE

- _____ beans with melted butter, sprinkled with an inquiry
  COLOR

  from your grandma if you're dating anyone _____ and a
  ADJECTIVE

  reminder that you're not _____ any younger.
  VERB ENDING IN "ING"

- _____ pie with a scoop of relief that you have another year
  NOUN

  until the next Thanks-_____!
  VERB ENDING IN "ING"

The world's greatest _party_ game

MAD LIBS® is fun to play with friends, but you can also play it by yourself! To begin with, DO NOT look at the story on the page below. Fill in the blanks on this page with the words called for. Then, using the words you have selected, fill in the blank spaces in the story. Now you've created your own hilarious MAD LIBS® game!

NOUN _____

PLURAL NOUN _____

NUMBER _____

VERB _____

ADJECTIVE _____

ADJECTIVE _____

A PLACE _____

ADJECTIVE _____

ADJECTIVE _____

VERB _____

NOUN _____

PART OF THE BODY _____

NOUN _____

NOUN _____

NOUN _____

VERB _____

NOUN _____

PLURAL NOUN _____

VERB ENDING IN "ING" _____

NOUN _____

ADJECTIVE _____

NOUN _____

Adult MAD LIBS — GRANDMA'S WILL

The world's greatest _party_ game

Dear Family, Well, I'm as dead as a/an _____ -nail. Don't be sad,
_{NOUN}

although I suspect some of you are thinking "Goody, goody gum-

_____ " at the thought of me _____ feet under. I, for one, am
_{PLURAL NOUN}   _{NUMBER}

excited to _____ through the _____ gates of Heaven and see
_{VERB}   _{ADJECTIVE}

my dearly departed poodle, Miss _____ -kins. As for Grandpa, we
_{ADJECTIVE}

all know he's rotting in (the) _____ , that dirty, _____ man.
_{A PLACE}   _{ADJECTIVE}

Now let's get down to the _____ stuff. To my disappointing son,
_{ADJECTIVE}

you need a good _____ in the face, not my money. Therefore, I
_{VERB}

bequeath you my state-of-the- _____ gym equipment. Get off your
_{NOUN}

_____ and do something. Also, you get my beach _____ in
_{PART OF THE BODY}   _{NOUN}

Boca. To my insufferable daughter, I give you my convertible _____.
_{NOUN}

You're quite dull—go on a cross- _____ trip and _____ it up
_{NOUN}   _{VERB}

already. Fine, have my diamond wedding _____ , too, even though
_{NOUN}

marriage isn't in the _____ for you. To my butler and maids, thanks
_{PLURAL NOUN}

for _____ to like me because I paid you to. You each get a set of
_{VERB ENDING IN "ING"}

sterling _____ flatware. And to my beloved cat, Mr. _____
_{NOUN}   _{ADJECTIVE}

Pants, the love of my life, you get the rest of my multimillion- _____
_{NOUN}

estate.

MAD LIBS® is fun to play with friends, but you can also play it by yourself! To begin with, DO NOT look at the story on the page below. Fill in the blanks on this page with the words called for. Then, using the words you have selected, fill in the blank spaces in the story. Now you've created your own hilarious MAD LIBS® game!

NOUN _____

ADJECTIVE _____

NOUN _____

PART OF THE BODY (PLURAL) _____

PLURAL NOUN _____

NOUN _____

NOUN _____

VERB _____

ADJECTIVE _____

NUMBER _____

VERB _____

PART OF THE BODY _____

PLURAL NOUN _____

VERB _____

NOUN _____

PART OF THE BODY _____

Adult MAD LIBS® ARE YOU THE LEAST FAVORITE?

The world's greatest _party_ game

Do your parents forget your birth-_____ every year? Are they

              NOUN

always bragging endlessly about how rich and _____ your older

                                ADJECTIVE

_____ is? Read this to see if you're the rotten apple of your

NOUN

parents' _____! You're the least favorite if . . .

   PART OF THE BODY (PLURAL)

All the presents you've ever given to your _____ wind up in the

                              PLURAL NOUN

attic. Or at the Salvation _____. Unable to wait until you went

                      NOUN

to college, your mom turned your childhood _____-room into

                            NOUN

her _____-in closet while you were still a senior. Your sister got

   VERB

a brand-_____ car for graduation. You got your dad's

            ADJECTIVE

_____-year-old station wagon. Your brother spent summers at

NUMBER

_____-away camp. You spent summers being bored out of your

VERB

_____ at Nana's. Your parents tell you "See you whenever!" when

PART OF THE BODY

you mention you're moving three thousand _____ away.

                        PLURAL NOUN

When you _____ up your folks, they always say "Who's this?"

         VERB

When you say "It's me!," they still don't have any _____ who you

                     NOUN

are. You see photos of a recent family vacation on _____-book.

                        PART OF THE BODY

Guess who wasn't invited? Surprise!

From ADULT MAD LIBS®: My Bleeping Family Mad Libs • Copyright © 2012 by Penguin Random House LLC.

MAD LIBS® is fun to play with friends, but you can also play it by yourself! To begin with, DO NOT look at the story on the page below. Fill in the blanks on this page with the words called for. Then, using the words you have selected, fill in the blank spaces in the story. Now you've created your own hilarious MAD LIBS® game!

NOUN _____

A PLACE _____

PART OF THE BODY _____

PERSON IN ROOM (FEMALE) _____

PART OF THE BODY (PLURAL) _____

NOUN _____

VERB ENDING IN "ING" _____

PLURAL NOUN _____

NOUN _____

SAME PERSON IN ROOM (FEMALE) _____

VERB ENDING IN "ING" _____

ADJECTIVE _____

VERB _____

PERSON IN ROOM (FEMALE) _____

VERB ENDING IN "ING" _____

PART OF THE BODY _____

ANIMAL _____

PLURAL NOUN _____

VERB _____

PERSON IN ROOM (FEMALE) _____

PERSON IN ROOM (FEMALE) _____

NOUN _____

VERB _____

Adult MAD LIBS

REALITY SHOW DRAMA

The world's greatest _party_ game

Did you miss the latest episode of *The Real* _____ -*wives of (the)*

NOUN

_____? Here's a recap of all the _____-stabbing behavior

A PLACE — PART OF THE BODY

you won't want to miss! So, remember how _____ wanted

PERSON IN ROOM (FEMALE)

to give her sixteen-year-old daughter a pair of double D _____

PART OF THE BODY (PLURAL)

for her birthday? Turns out her dad is being sued for _____

NOUN

evasion and the bank is fore-_____ on their house! The girl

VERB ENDING IN "ING"

threw a hissy fit and cried buckets of _____. No plastic

PLURAL NOUN

_____ for anyone, so sad! But wait! _____ is sweet-

NOUN — SAME PERSON IN ROOM (FEMALE)

_____ the doctor into a discount. So maybe this tale will have

VERB ENDING IN "ING"

a/an _____ ending after all! Then, the single and ready-to-

ADJECTIVE

_____ _____ was seen _____ up a storm with the

VERB — PERSON IN ROOM (FEMALE) — VERB ENDING IN "ING"

husband of her boss. "You know where to find me if you ever need

company," she whispered in his _____. Risky! Of course, no

PART OF THE BODY

episode is complete without a/an _____-fight between two so-

ANIMAL

called best _____. At an '80s _____-up party, _____

PLURAL NOUN — VERB — PERSON IN ROOM (FEMALE)

called _____ a "fashion _____." Meow! Don't forget to

PERSON IN ROOM (FEMALE) — NOUN

_____ in next week!

VERB

From ADULT MAD LIBS®: My Bleeping Family Mad Libs • Copyright © 2012 by Penguin Random House LLC.

Adult MAD LIBS

VISITING THE IN-LAWS: A GUIDE

The world's greatest _party_ game

MAD LIBS® is fun to play with friends, but you can also play it by yourself! To begin with, DO NOT look at the story on the page below. Fill in the blanks on this page with the words called for. Then, using the words you have selected, fill in the blank spaces in the story. Now you've created your own hilarious MAD LIBS® game!

ADJECTIVE _____

NOUN _____

ADJECTIVE _____

ADJECTIVE _____

VERB ENDING IN "ING" _____

NOUN _____

NOUN _____

VERB _____

NOUN _____

ADJECTIVE _____

ADJECTIVE _____

PLURAL NOUN _____

PART OF THE BODY _____

PLURAL NOUN _____

LETTER OF THE ALPHABET _____

VERB _____

VERB _____

NOUN _____

NOUN _____

Adult MAD LIBS

VISITING THE IN-LAWS: A GUIDE

The world's greatest __*party*__ game

Yay, it's that _____ time of year when you and the ol' ball and

ADJECTIVE

_____ get to visit your _____ in-laws. Here are some

NOUN · ADJECTIVE

tried-and-_____ tips on how to survive without _____

ADJECTIVE · VERB ENDING IN "ING"

anyone! Do the in-laws not believe in _____ locks? Or knocking

NOUN

on the _____-room door before coming in? Bring your own "Do

NOUN

not _____" sign and hang it wherever you need privacy. If they

VERB

keep bugging you to have a/an _____ so they can be _____-

NOUN · ADJECTIVE

parents, tell them you're pregnant—who cares if it's a big _____

ADJECTIVE

lie? If your mother-in-law's cooking makes your taste-_____ beg

PLURAL NOUN

for mercy, explain you came down with a terrible _____ bug.

PART OF THE BODY

Then sneak out later for a hamburger and french _____! Does

PLURAL NOUN

your father-in-law love telling _____-rated jokes that make

LETTER OF THE ALPHABET

you cringe? Or worse, corny ones that make only him _____ a

VERB

gut? Tell him he should be a/an _____-up comedian. And if he

VERB

says, "Really?" smile and say no. Lastly, if your in-laws give you a guilt

_____ for not visiting enough, suggest they pay for your air-

NOUN

_____ tickets next time. That'll keep 'em quiet!

NOUN

MAD LIBS® is fun to play with friends, but you can also play it by yourself! To begin with, DO NOT look at the story on the page below. Fill in the blanks on this page with the words called for. Then, using the words you have selected, fill in the blank spaces in the story. Now you've created your own hilarious MAD LIBS® game!

ADJECTIVE _____

PLURAL NOUN _____

NOUN _____

VERB _____

VERB _____

PART OF THE BODY _____

NOUN _____

PLURAL NOUN _____

PART OF THE BODY (PLURAL) _____

NOUN _____

PLURAL NOUN _____

VERB (PAST TENSE) _____

PART OF THE BODY _____

VERB _____

ADJECTIVE _____

PLURAL NOUN _____

NOUN _____

PLURAL NOUN _____

VERB ENDING IN "ING" _____

Congratulations! You and your sweetie have welcomed a/an

_____-born baby into your family. Now that you're home from
_{ADJECTIVE}

the hospital with your bundle of _____, here are some tips on
_{PLURAL NOUN}

surviving new _____-hood! First, tiny humans mainly do three
_{NOUN}

things all day long: eat, sleep, and _____ like there's no tomorrow.
_{VERB}

Be prepared to have _____-up stains on most of your clothes. If
_{VERB}

your wife is _____-feeding, make sure she has a comfortable
_{PART OF THE BODY}

chair to sit in and a glass of _____ should she get thirsty. And
_{NOUN}

gentle-_____, hands off her _____ while the baby's
_{PLURAL NOUN}   _{PART OF THE BODY (PLURAL)}

eating. For many new moms, the idea of a steamy roll in the _____
_{NOUN}

is the last thing on her mind. Are you getting into petty _____
_{PLURAL NOUN}

with each other because you haven't _____ in days? A good rule
_{VERB (PAST TENSE)}

of _____ is to _____ when your _____ angel sleeps.
_{PART OF THE BODY}   _{VERB}   _{ADJECTIVE}

You'll still be a pair of walking _____, but less prone to snapping
_{PLURAL NOUN}

at each other at the drop of a/an _____. Knee-deep in changing
_{NOUN}

dirty _____? Babies are _____ machines, so it's only fair to
_{PLURAL NOUN}   _{VERB ENDING IN "ING"}

take turns!

Adult MAD LIBS

BIRTHDAY DINNER INVITATION

The world's greatest _party_ game

MAD LIBS® is fun to play with friends, but you can also play it by yourself! To begin with, DO NOT look at the story on the page below. Fill in the blanks on this page with the words called for. Then, using the words you have selected, fill in the blank spaces in the story. Now you've created your own hilarious MAD LIBS® game!

PLURAL NOUN _____

PERSON IN ROOM (MALE) _____

SAME PERSON IN ROOM (MALE) _____

ADJECTIVE _____

NOUN _____

NOUN _____

VERB ENDING IN "ING" _____

PLURAL NOUN _____

VERB ENDING IN "ING" _____

NOUN _____

NOUN _____

NOUN _____

NOUN _____

PLURAL NOUN _____

PLURAL NOUN _____

ADJECTIVE _____

PART OF THE BODY _____

VERB (PAST TENSE) _____

Adult MAD LIBS® — BIRTHDAY DINNER INVITATION

The world's greatest _party_ game

Dear Family and _____, you are invited to the surprise birthday
<small>PLURAL NOUN</small>

of my father, _____ Von _____. Many of you know
<small>PERSON IN ROOM (MALE)</small>   <small>SAME PERSON IN ROOM (MALE)</small>

him by his nickname, "Ol' _____ _____," though I refer
<small>ADJECTIVE</small>   <small>NOUN</small>

to him as "the man who ignored me my entire life because he was too

busy building his _____ empire, _____ on my mom with
<small>NOUN</small>   <small>VERB ENDING IN "ING"</small>

his rotating cast of pretty _____, and _____ endless rounds of
<small>PLURAL NOUN</small>   <small>VERB ENDING IN "ING"</small>

golf." There is so much to celebrate about my absentee _____! Like
<small>NOUN</small>

the way he never came to a single base-_____ game I played. Or
<small>NOUN</small>

when he refused to pay for college when he found out I was majoring

in art _____. And then there was the time he hit on my
<small>NOUN</small>

_____ at our engagement party after a few too many gin and
<small>NOUN</small>

_____. What an appetite for life he has! Let us gather at Royal
<small>PLURAL NOUN</small>

_____ Country Club to honor this person who some of us love.
<small>PLURAL NOUN</small>

Though he has a/an _____ heart and may very well suffer a/an
<small>ADJECTIVE</small>

_____ attack at the excitement of the occasion, please keep your
<small>PART OF THE BODY</small>

lips _____. We wouldn't want to spoil it for the guest of dishonor!
<small>VERB (PAST TENSE)</small>

From ADULT MAD LIBS®: My Bleeping Family Mad Libs • Copyright © 2012 by Penguin Random House LLC.

THE BLACK SHEEP

The world's greatest _party_ game

MAD LIBS® is fun to play with friends, but you can also play it by yourself! To begin with, DO NOT look at the story on the page below. Fill in the blanks on this page with the words called for. Then, using the words you have selected, fill in the blank spaces in the story. Now you've created your own hilarious MAD LIBS® game!

COLOR _____

VERB _____

PERSON IN ROOM (FEMALE) _____

VERB ENDING IN "ING" _____

NOUN _____

NUMBER _____

ADJECTIVE _____

NOUN _____

VERB _____

VERB ENDING IN "ING" _____

NOUN _____

NOUN _____

NOUN _____

NOUN _____

PART OF THE BODY _____

VERB (PAST TENSE) _____

PLURAL NOUN _____

NOUN _____

Are you the _____ sheep in your family like I am? Then you

COLOR

know how it feels to have everyone _____ up against you and

VERB

then have the nerve to call you "Greedy Aunt _____" when

PERSON IN ROOM (FEMALE)

they think you aren't _____ attention. Well, duh, I sure do have

VERB ENDING IN "ING"

a/an _____ in my bonnet if you're talking trash about me! Okay,

NOUN

so once I borrowed _____ thousand dollars from my _____-

NUMBER   ADJECTIVE

mother and didn't pay her back. When she kicked the _____,

NOUN

may she _____ in peace, my parents deducted the amount from

VERB

my inheritance. I said "Are you _____ kidding me? Grandma

VERB ENDING IN "ING"

would roll over in her _____ if she knew what you did!" Then,

NOUN

they called me a "klepto-_____" and a/an "_____-lifter"

NOUN   NOUN

because I also happened to have her pearl _____ and matching

NOUN

_____-rings. But I swear Grandma gave them to me! Well, I

PART OF THE BODY

know she would've if she hadn't _____ her marbles before then.

VERB (PAST TENSE)

She loved me to bits and _____ and would have wanted me to

PLURAL NOUN

have them! Now, whenever I see my family, they watch me like a/an

_____. Life's so unfair, am I right?

NOUN

Adult MAD LIBS

MOVING BACK IN WITH YOUR PARENTS: A GUIDE

The world's greatest _party_ game

MAD LIBS® is fun to play with friends, but you can also play it by yourself! To begin with, DO NOT look at the story on the page below. Fill in the blanks on this page with the words called for. Then, using the words you have selected, fill in the blank spaces in the story. Now you've created your own hilarious MAD LIBS® game!

NOUN _____

NOUN _____

NOUN _____

PART OF THE BODY _____

NUMBER _____

PLURAL NOUN _____

PART OF THE BODY (PLURAL) _____

ADJECTIVE _____

VERB ENDING IN "ING" _____

NOUN _____

PLURAL NOUN _____

ADJECTIVE _____

VERB ENDING IN "ING" _____

NOUN _____

VERB ENDING IN "ING" _____

NOUN _____

VERB _____

NOUN _____

NOUN _____

PLURAL NOUN _____

VERB ENDING IN "ING" _____

ADJECTIVE _____

Adult MAD LIBS
MOVING BACK IN WITH YOUR PARENTS: A GUIDE

The world's greatest _party_ game

So, you lost your full-time _____ and can't pay the land-
<small>NOUN</small>

_____ ? Welcome home! Your childhood bedroom awaits. But
<small>NOUN</small>

before you settle in to your twin-size _____ , keep these rules in
<small>NOUN</small>

the back of your _____ or you could end up living there for the
<small>PART OF THE BODY</small>

next _____ years:
<small>NUMBER</small>

1. Never tell potential love _____ about your situation. If
<small>PLURAL NOUN</small>

   necessary, lie through your _____ and just say "Oh, those
   <small>PART OF THE BODY (PLURAL)</small>

   _____ people? Roommates!" It goes without _____
   <small>ADJECTIVE</small>   <small>VERB ENDING IN "ING"</small>

   that bringing dates home is a recipe for _____ .
   <small>NOUN</small>

2. Sure, eating mom's delicious meat-_____ and having a
   <small>PLURAL NOUN</small>

   bathroom with a non-_____ shower curtain make you feel
   <small>ADJECTIVE</small>

   like you're _____large. But don't forget, at the end of the
   <small>VERB ENDING IN "ING"</small>

   _____ , you're still_____ under the same _____
   <small>NOUN</small>   <small>VERB ENDING IN "ING"</small>   <small>NOUN</small>

   as the folks that taught you how to _____ in a toilet. Aspire
   <small>VERB</small>

   to afford cable _____ for your own place one day!
   <small>NOUN</small>

3. Do your parents give you a weekly _____to do chores like
   <small>NOUN</small>

   cleaning the _____and _____ out the garbage? Hey,
   <small>PLURAL NOUN</small>   <small>VERB ENDING IN "ING"</small>

   maybe living at home isn't so _____ after all!
   <small>ADJECTIVE</small>

DEAR DIARY

The world's greatest _party_ game

MAD LIBS® is fun to play with friends, but you can also play it by yourself! To begin with, DO NOT look at the story on the page below. Fill in the blanks on this page with the words called for. Then, using the words you have selected, fill in the blank spaces in the story. Now you've created your own hilarious MAD LIBS® game!

ADJECTIVE _____

PLURAL NOUN _____

VERB _____

NOUN _____

VERB ENDING IN "ING" _____

PERSON IN ROOM (MALE) _____

VERB _____

SAME PERSON IN ROOM (MALE) _____

PART OF THE BODY (PLURAL) _____

VERB _____

NOUN _____

PART OF THE BODY (PLURAL) _____

ADJECTIVE _____

VERB ENDING IN "ING" _____

NOUN _____

PLURAL NOUN _____

NOUN _____

VERB ENDING IN "ING" _____

VERB _____

Adult MAD LIBS — DEAR DIARY

The world's greatest _party_ game

Read an entry from your teenage diary about that time Dad chaperoned

the _____ school dance and became the center of attention with
     ADJECTIVE

his smooth _____!
            PLURAL NOUN

Dear Diary,

I so need to _____ out of school and go into a/an _____
              VERB   NOUN

protection program after what happened last night. There I was, slow-

_____ with _____ to "I Will Always _____ You." I
VERB ENDING IN "ING"   PERSON IN ROOM (MALE)   VERB

didn't even care that Dad was there because I finally had _____'s
                                                          SAME PERSON IN ROOM (MALE)

_____ wrapped around me. Heaven! Then, Britney's
PART OF THE BODY (PLURAL)

"_____ Me _____ One More Time" came on, and Dad
   VERB   NOUN

literally went nuts. He put his _____ in the air and busted
                                PART OF THE BODY (PLURAL)

out his _____ school moves: the _____ Man, the
        ADJECTIVE   VERB ENDING IN "ING"

_____ Patch, and the Sprinkler. A circle of _____
NOUN   PLURAL NOUN

formed around him, chanting "You Go, Old _____!" I wanted
                                         NOUN

to kill him. The saddest part? He thought people were laughing with

him, but they were _____ at him. I'm, like, never going to
                   VERB ENDING IN "ING"

_____ this down. Ever!
VERB

MAD LIBS® is fun to play with friends, but you can also play it by yourself! To begin with, DO NOT look at the story on the page below. Fill in the blanks on this page with the words called for. Then, using the words you have selected, fill in the blank spaces in the story. Now you've created your own hilarious MAD LIBS® game!

NOUN _____

PART OF THE BODY _____

ADJECTIVE _____

NOUN _____

ADJECTIVE _____

PART OF THE BODY _____

VERB _____

NOUN _____

ADJECTIVE _____

PLURAL NOUN _____

NOUN _____

ADJECTIVE _____

ADJECTIVE _____

PART OF THE BODY _____

VERB _____

VERB _____

PLURAL NOUN _____

Adult MAD LIBS
SECRET SANTA

The world's greatest _party_ game

Buying Christmas presents for every family _____ is not only

<small>NOUN</small>

stressful but also costs an arm and a/an _____ . Which is why

<small>PART OF THE BODY</small>

doing Secret Santa can seem like a/an _____ option. That way,

<small>ADJECTIVE</small>

everyone picks a/an _____ from a hat and buys that person a

<small>NOUN</small>

gift. Simple, right? But be warned! _____ Santa can really

<small>ADJECTIVE</small>

_____-fire if, like most of us, you like to re-_____ presents

<small>PART OF THE BODY</small>   <small>VERB</small>

from previous years. There's nothing wrong with "recycling" that

useless _____-maker your aunt got you or the _____

<small>NOUN</small>   <small>ADJECTIVE</small>

edition plate set of the US _____ that Grandpa thought was right

<small>PLURAL NOUN</small>

up your _____ . Unless you end up wrapping that present like it

<small>NOUN</small>

is brand-_____ and giving it to the person who originally gave

<small>ADJECTIVE</small>

it to you. Ooops! Should this happen, you must absolutely tell a big

_____ lie that you _____-picked the gift just for them.

<small>ADJECTIVE</small>   <small>PART OF THE BODY</small>

They may not believe a word you _____ , but you really don't

<small>VERB</small>

have a choice. To avoid this scenario, make sure you _____ down

<small>VERB</small>

who gave you what unwanted item. As long as you keep track of them,

bad _____ are the gift that you keep giving . . . to someone else!

<small>PLURAL NOUN</small>

The world's greatest _party_ game

MAD LIBS® is fun to play with friends, but you can also play it by yourself! To begin with, DO NOT look at the story on the page below. Fill in the blanks on this page with the words called for. Then, using the words you have selected, fill in the blank spaces in the story. Now you've created your own hilarious MAD LIBS® game!

NOUN _____

ADJECTIVE _____

NOUN _____

PERSON IN ROOM (FEMALE) _____

NOUN _____

NOUN _____

ADJECTIVE _____

VERB _____

PLURAL NOUN _____

NOUN _____

PART OF THE BODY _____

NOUN _____

NOUN _____

NOUN _____

NOUN _____

Some people in my family think all I do is gab about them, like I have

nothing better to do with my precious _____. I mean, really?
NOUN

Like I live for airing everyone's _____ laundry. Please. I would
ADJECTIVE

never gossip about how my _____-in-law, _____, told
NOUN   PERSON IN ROOM (FEMALE)

my husband that she's thinking of sending her grandson to a psycho-

_____. Well, it's about time. That kid has more issues than I do
NOUN

of _Celebrity_ _____ magazine—and I'm a subscriber! And besides
NOUN

my _____ circle of friends and a few strangers in the
ADJECTIVE

_____-out line at the grocery store, have I ever told anyone how
VERB

my mother-in-law gave her other grand-_____ cars for their
PLURAL NOUN

sixteenth birthdays, but all of a sudden has "run out of _____"
NOUN

to give one to my daughter? No! I just bite my _____ and keep it
PART OF THE BODY

inside. Why would I ever want anyone to know that my husband got a

substantial _____ from his boss, but no one else did? Or that the
NOUN

real reason my aunt divorced my uncle is because she's been secretly in

the _____ all these years! That's nobody's _____ but her
NOUN   NOUN

own. Of course I had to mention it to my massage _____, but
NOUN

she's practically family!

Adult

MAD LIBS

DYSFUNCTIONAL FAMOUS FAMILIES: A CHECKLIST

The world's greatest _party_ game

MAD LIBS® is fun to play with friends, but you can also play it by yourself! To begin with, DO NOT look at the story on the page below. Fill in the blanks on this page with the words called for. Then, using the words you have selected, fill in the blank spaces in the story. Now you've created your own hilarious MAD LIBS® game!

ADJECTIVE _____

PLURAL NOUN _____

VERB ENDING IN "ING" _____

NOUN _____

VERB (PAST TENSE) _____

NOUN _____

VERB _____

NOUN _____

NUMBER _____

NOUN _____

VERB ENDING IN "ING" _____

NUMBER _____

VERB _____

NOUN _____

NOUN _____

NOUN _____

VERB (PAST TENSE) _____

A PLACE _____

You know you grew up in a/an _____-known dysfunctional
ADJECTIVE

family when:

- Your dad was the president of the United _____ and got caught
PLURAL NOUN

  _____ the hot _____. Extra points if he _____ about
  VERB ENDING IN "ING" NOUN VERB (PAST TENSE)

  it on national _____.
  NOUN

- Your manager mother thinks it's a good idea for you to _____
  VERB

  naked in *Play-*_____.
  NOUN

- She also thinks you need to lose ten to _____ pounds so you
  NUMBER

  can land that diet _____ deal.
  NOUN

- Your sister is constantly in and out of rehab for exhaustion and

  addiction to _____ pills. The luxurious facility could double
  VERB ENDING IN "ING"

  as a/an _____-star spa.
  NUMBER

- Your dad is a rock 'n' _____ star who fathered several children
  VERB

  throughout his career. You didn't find out he was your biological

  _____ until you saw it on the front page of the news-_____.
  NOUN NOUN

- You and your brothers were in a/an _____-band group and your
  NOUN

  parents _____ all your money. You had to sue them in (the)
  VERB (PAST TENSE)

  _____ to get your earnings back.
  A PLACE

MAD LIBS® is fun to play with friends, but you can also play it by yourself! To begin with, DO NOT look at the story on the page below. Fill in the blanks on this page with the words called for. Then, using the words you have selected, fill in the blank spaces in the story. Now you've created your own hilarious MAD LIBS® game!

VERB ENDING IN "ING" _____

NOUN _____

ADJECTIVE _____

PART OF THE BODY _____

VERB _____

VERB _____

PLURAL NOUN _____

ADJECTIVE _____

VERB _____

NOUN _____

VERB ENDING IN "ING" _____

VERB _____

VERB ENDING IN "ING" _____

PLURAL NOUN _____

NOUN _____

NUMBER _____

VERB ENDING IN "ING" _____

NOUN _____

NOUN _____

So your kids are all _____ on their own and now it's just you and
_{VERB ENDING IN "ING"}

your partner all alone in an empty _____? Check out this guide
_{NOUN}

for _____ nesters on how to live with your sweet-_____,
_{ADJECTIVE} _{PART OF THE BODY}

even if you _____ each other to death! First and foremost, make
_{VERB}

sure you each _____ out a part of the house to call your own.
_{VERB}

Ideally, these territories should be on different _____. This way
_{PLURAL NOUN}

it's possible to go a/an _____ stretch of the day without having to
_{ADJECTIVE}

actually_____ each other. You can always stay in touch by speaker-
_{VERB}

_____ or instant _____! And then regroup at dinner to
_{NOUN} _{VERB ENDING IN "ING"}

_____ up on all the things you didn't do together that day. Tired
_{VERB}

of his constant _____ at night? Now you have more bed-
_{VERB ENDING IN "ING"}

_____to use, so you can fall asleep anywhere! If you find that you
_{PLURAL NOUN}

don't have anything in common with the _____ you married
_{NOUN}

besides your_____ offspring, try a new hobby together. Something
_{NUMBER}

as simple as taking a/an _____ or _____-watching class can
_{VERB ENDING IN "ING"} _{NOUN}

really reignite the _____. If not, just pretend it does for the sake
_{NOUN}

of your_____!
_{PLURAL NOUN}

Adult MAD LIBS® SO WHAT, I'M A COUGAR!

The world's greatest _party_ game

MAD LIBS® is fun to play with friends, but you can also play it by yourself! To begin with, DO NOT look at the story on the page below. Fill in the blanks on this page with the words called for. Then, using the words you have selected, fill in the blank spaces in the story. Now you've created your own hilarious MAD LIBS® game!

NOUN _____

ADJECTIVE _____

VERB ENDING IN "ING" _____

NOUN _____

NUMBER _____

ANIMAL _____

PLURAL NOUN _____

VERB _____

VERB _____

ADJECTIVE _____

VERB _____

PLURAL NOUN _____

VERB _____

ADJECTIVE _____

VERB (PAST TENSE) _____

PLURAL NOUN _____

ADJECTIVE _____

PLURAL NOUN _____

PART OF THE BODY _____

VERB ENDING IN "ING"

Adult MAD LIBS

SO WHAT, I'M A COUGAR!

The world's greatest _party_ game

Are you an older, single _____ who finds men your age a/an
                  NOUN

_____ snoozefest? Take it from me that_____younger guys
ADJECTIVE   VERB ENDING IN "ING"

can do wonders for your _____ life! After divorcing my ex after
                            NOUN

_____ decades of marriage, I thought I'd be alone forever. Then I
NUMBER

found a dating website called _____-love.com that matches
                               ANIMAL

women like me with _____who like older ladies. I figured, why
                       PLURAL NOUN

not? I have nothing to lose and everything to_____. One thing is
                                    VERB

for sure, these men are eager to _____ you. All they want is to
                           VERB

make you feel _____! They don't _____ around baggage or
          ADJECTIVE   VERB

have_____ to worry about. This one guy loved to role-_____—
    PLURAL NOUN   VERB

we pretended I was his teacher and he was the _____ student.
                                    ADJECTIVE

Naughty! I've even _____up with one of my daughter's college
            VERB (PAST TENSE)

_____. Unfortunately, she found out and is no longer speaking to
PLURAL NOUN

me. What can I say, I was blinded by_____lust! With his ripped,
                              ADJECTIVE

lean _____and full _____ of hair, I couldn't resist. Truth?
   PLURAL NOUN   PART OF THE BODY

We've been _____ each other in secret. Double naughty!
      VERB ENDING IN "ING"

Adult

MAD LIBS A ROYAL MESS

The world's greatest _party_ game

MAD LIBS® is fun to play with friends, but you can also play it by yourself! To begin with, DO NOT look at the story on the page below. Fill in the blanks on this page with the words called for. Then, using the words you have selected, fill in the blank spaces in the story. Now you've created your own hilarious MAD LIBS® game!

PLURAL NOUN _____

ADJECTIVE _____

CELEBRITY (MALE) _____

CELEBRITY (FEMALE) _____

NOUN _____

ADJECTIVE _____

NUMBER _____

PART OF THE BODY (PLURAL) _____

VERB ENDING IN "ING" _____

ADJECTIVE _____

PLURAL NOUN _____

PLURAL NOUN _____

VERB (PAST TENSE) _____

PART OF THE BODY (PLURAL) _____

ADJECTIVE _____

COLOR _____

PERSON IN ROOM (MALE) _____

PART OF THE BODY _____

Adult MAD LIBS
A ROYAL MESS

The world's greatest __party__ game

Throughout the ages, royal _____ have been fraught with some

PLURAL NOUN

seriously _____ dysfunction. Let's take a look, shall we? In recent

ADJECTIVE

times, Prince _____ of England notoriously cheated on his wife,

CELEBRITY (MALE)

Lady _____, with his mistress. In turn, she found solace in the

CELEBRITY (FEMALE)

arms of a sympathetic _____. Touché! In the 1500s, one of the

NOUN

most _____ English kings was Henry VIII. Out of his _____

ADJECTIVE   NUMBER

wives, two had their _____ chopped off under his command.

PART OF THE BODY (PLURAL)

Yikes! Many royals practiced in-_____ to keep their family lines

VERB ENDING IN "ING"

_____ and clean. In ancient Egypt, pharaohs married their own

ADJECTIVE

_____. In Britain, it was common for first _____ to marry.

PLURAL NOUN   PLURAL NOUN

The Habsburgs inter-_____ so much that a genetic disorder

VERB (PAST TENSE)

developed where their _____ didn't function correctly.

PART OF THE BODY (PLURAL)

Another _____ thing about _____ bloods is that they often

ADJECTIVE   COLOR

like to be in the spotlight. For instance, _____ XIV

PERSON IN ROOM (MALE)

enjoyed having his _____ cleaned while holding court. If that's

PART OF THE BODY

called _____ the royal treatment, I think I'll pass!

VERB ENDING IN "ING"

From ADULT MAD LIBS®: My Bleeping Family Mad Libs • Copyright © 2012 by Penguin Random House LLC.

Adult MAD LIBS — MY NOT-SO-EVIL STEPMOM

The world's greatest _party_ game

MAD LIBS® is fun to play with friends, but you can also play it by yourself! To begin with, DO NOT look at the story on the page below. Fill in the blanks on this page with the words called for. Then, using the words you have selected, fill in the blank spaces in the story. Now you've created your own hilarious MAD LIBS® game!

NOUN _____

NOUN _____

ADVERB _____

NOUN _____

PERSON IN ROOM (FEMALE) _____

NOUN _____

PLURAL NOUN _____

ADJECTIVE _____

NOUN _____

PLURAL NOUN _____

VERB (PAST TENSE) _____

A PLACE _____

PART OF THE BODY (PLURAL) _____

VERB _____

PLURAL NOUN _____

ADJECTIVE _____

VERB _____

SAME PERSON IN ROOM (FEMALE) _____

VERB _____

NOUN _____

ADJECTIVE _____

NOUN

My dad's on his second _____, and boy is she a/an _____! I
NOUN   NOUN

really wanted to find something _____ wrong with her, but she's
ADVERB

sweet as _____. Truthfully, _____ is a lot nicer than my
NOUN   PERSON IN ROOM (FEMALE)

real mom. I was hoping for a Cinderella situation, where I triumph

over my evil step-_____, but even her two _____ are
NOUN   PLURAL NOUN

ridiculously _____. One of them even set me up with a cute
ADJECTIVE

_____! We all get along like gang-_____. She and my dad
NOUN   PLURAL NOUN

_____ on a singles cruise to (the) _____. I could tell she
VERB (PAST TENSE)   A PLACE

made him happy by the way his _____ lit up every time he
PART OF THE BODY (PLURAL)

mentioned her. I was ready to _____ her guts the first time we
VERB

met. But then she brought me a box of my favorite_____. I could
PLURAL NOUN

complain that she's almost too _____ and thoughtful! My mom
ADJECTIVE

likes to _____whatever I say about her into something negative.
VERB

Like if_____ gives me a present, my mom will say, "Oh,
SAME PERSON IN ROOM (FEMALE)

she's just trying to _____ your love. It's the oldest trick in the
VERB

_____." I think if she remarries, my mom is going to be the most
NOUN

_____ stepmother ever. I already feel sorry for her future boy-_____.
ADJECTIVE   NOUN

Adult MAD LIBS® KISSING COUSINS

The world's greatest _party_ game

MAD LIBS® is fun to play with friends, but you can also play it by yourself! To begin with, DO NOT look at the story on the page below. Fill in the blanks on this page with the words called for. Then, using the words you have selected, fill in the blank spaces in the story. Now you've created your own hilarious MAD LIBS® game!

ADJECTIVE _____

VERB ENDING IN "ING" _____

PERSON IN ROOM (FEMALE) _____

VERB _____

PLURAL NOUN _____

NUMBER _____

PLURAL NOUN _____

NOUN _____

NOUN _____

PART OF THE BODY (PLURAL) _____

NOUN _____

PLURAL NOUN _____

ADJECTIVE _____

NOUN _____

ADJECTIVE _____

PLURAL NOUN _____

VERB _____

PART OF THE BODY _____

VERB _____

COLOR _____

NOUN _____

ADJECTIVE

Adult MAD LIBS KISSING COUSINS

The world's greatest _party_ game

To My One _____ Love,
ADJECTIVE

Oh, how I am _____ for you! Like Romeo and _____,
VERB ENDING IN "ING" _PERSON IN ROOM (FEMALE)_

what a cruel _____ of fate that we are star-crossed _____!
VERB _PLURAL NOUN_

Who cares that we share _____ percent of the same DNA? The
NUMBER

royals do it all the time! Ever since we were little _____, I always
PLURAL NOUN

felt like we were two peas in a/an _____. Do you remember when
NOUN

we were eight years old and went to _____-world? We held
NOUN

_____ during the entire roller-_____ ride. It sent
PART OF THE BODY (PLURAL) _NOUN_

_____ up my spine! When we got older, I would always get
PLURAL NOUN

_____ when you talked about your high school _____-friend.
ADJECTIVE _NOUN_

And now, I can't stop thinking about the _____ kiss we shared at
ADJECTIVE

last week's family reunion. So what that our _____ are brother and
PLURAL NOUN

sister? _____ taboos! I know in my _____ we're meant to be
VERB _PART OF THE BODY_

together. Do you _____ the same way? I hope it wasn't just the
VERB

_____ wine talking when you told me I am your _____-mate.
COLOR _NOUN_

My dream is one day we'll be able to share our secret love with the

whole _____ world!
ADJECTIVE

Download Mad Libs today!

Join the millions of Mad Libs fans creating wacky and wonderful stories on our apps!